THE
Dallas
Cowboys

Previous books by Leonard Shapiro

The Washington Redskins
Big Man on Campus:
John Thompson and the Georgetown Hoyas
Tough Stuff: The Man in the Middle (with Sam Huff)
Athletes for Sale (with Ken Denlinger)

THE
Dallas
Cowboys

Leonard Shapiro

ST. MARTIN'S PRESS NEW YORK

Library of Congress Cataloging-in-Publication Data

Shapiro, Leonard.
    The Dallas Cowboys / Leonard Shapiro.
        p.   cm.
    ISBN 0-312-09796-4
    1. Dallas Cowboys (Football team)—History. 2. Dallas Cowboys (Football team)—Miscellanea. I. Title.
    GV956.D3S53   1993
    796.332′64′097642812—dc20   93-14368
                                                                             CIP

First Edition: October 1993
10 9 8 7 6 5 4 3 2 1

To Vicky, for all her love, to Jennifer, Emily and Taylor, for all the joy, to Eric and David, for always being there, to Mom and Pop, for everything.

CONTENTS

ACKNOWLEDGMENTS

Once again, many thanks to all my friends and colleagues at *The Washington Post,* particularly Assistant Managing Editor George Solomon; Richard Justice, the hardest-working reporter I know; Ken Denlinger, a treasured collaborator on so many projects over the years; and Gene Wang, a Cowboy-lover forever. Also thanks to the Dallas Cowboys present, from owner Jerry Jones to public relations director Rich Dalrymple, and to Dallas Cowboys past, especially Tex Schramm, a football visionary. Thanks also to my agent and dear friend, Esther Newberg, and my favorite editor at St. Martin's, George Witte.

INTRODUCTION

Back when the Dallas Cowboys first slipped into my consciousness, they were not quite yet America's Team, even though they'd already won their first Super Bowl and would challenge for four more over the next two decades.

The year was 1973, my first covering the Cowboys' hated rivals, the Washington Redskins, as a beat reporter on *The Washington Post.* Oh my how the Redskins loved to hate the guys in silver and blue, how they'd taunt them from long distance, how they'd mock their computer offense, how Redskin coach George Allen would wander through his backyard telling his sons, "If I get this weed out in one piece, we'll beat the Cowboys next week."

One shining moment still remains etched in my memory bank. It was Monday night, October 8, 1973, my first Redskin-Cowboy game at RFK Stadium in Washington. It was a typically hard-fought affair, and in the end, it came down to one of the greatest defensive plays I've ever seen.

The Cowboys were trailing, 14–7, but were driving toward the Redskin goal line in the final minute of play. They had one last chance inside the five-yard line, and when the ball was handed off to rough-tough Walt Garrison, for a brief moment it appeared the big Cowboy running back had an open field to a touchdown.

But wait. From his position at strong safety, Hall of Famer Ken Houston glided into the play and literally lassoed Garrison, a rodeo cowboy in the off-season, and wrestled him to the ground inches short to save the score, to save the game.

At that moment, a roar came up from the crowd the likes of which I've never experienced before or since. Now, 54,000 fans were standing, stomping their feet so hard the press box

I sat in actually swayed back and forth as if an earthquake had shifted the very foundation of the stadium.

There were many more games like that over the years, and to tell the truth, I've always had a special feeling for the team Washington has always loathed.

It had a lot to do with the people. Calvin Hill was a joy to interview then, a good friend now. Roger Staubach was the most cooperative and unassuming superstar quarterback in the history of the league. I even got the silent one, Duane Thomas, into an animated conversation a few years later when he tried to sell me an insurance policy.

No matter how big the game, no matter how high the stakes, I can never recall Tom Landry not returning a telephone call. Or Tex Schramm. Or Gil Brandt. And especially not Jerry Jones, the high-energy new owner who has clearly made good on his promise to rebuild the franchise to live up to the legacy of one of the proudest teams in the National Football League.

Now, thirty-three years after Clint Murchison, Jr., was granted an expansion franchise that didn't win a game that first 1960 season, the Dallas Cowboys are nothing less than an institution, both in Texas and across the country. And of course, they are world champions once again, the only team ever to appear in six Super Bowls.

So why not a book of trivia on this storied team, even if it is authored by a man from the so-called enemy camp? Not really.

No, I've always been a closet Cowboy man, and so I give you three hundred trivia questions—a few no-brainers, a few toughies, and some more that may send you to the history books—to test your knowledge and jar your memory of Cowboys past and present (and a few old Redskins, just for good measure).

—Leonard Shapiro
September 1993

WARM-UP

1 Jerry Jones and Jimmy Johnson were teammates on a national championship college team. Name the school and the year.

•

2 What were two of Roger Staubach's nicknames when he played for the Cowboys?

•

3 What former NFL quarterback was a high school teammate of wide receiver Drew Pearson in New Jersey?

•

4 What former Cowboy linebacker helped pro golfer John Daly through an alcohol rehabilitation program?

•

5 What former Cowboy running back is the father of a two-time NCAA basketball champion?

•

6 What long-time assistant coach in the Tom Landry era was a Hall of Fame defensive lineman for the Pittsburgh Steelers?

•

7 What former Cowboy quarterback will forever be known for throwing a last-minute touchdown pass to beat the Washington Redskins on Thanksgiving Day 1974?

•

8 What player holds the team record for longest kickoff return?

•

9 What defensive lineman was known as "The Manster," half man, half monster?

•

3

10 Who is the only Cowboy to fly missions over Iraq during the Gulf War?

•

11 Troy Aikman grew up in Cerritos, California, but earned all-state honors at what Oklahoma high school?

•

12 Who was Clint Murchison's original partner when Dallas was awarded an NFL expansion franchise in 1960?

•

13 Name the four Cowboys in the Hall of Fame and a fifth Hall of Famer who played in Dallas but spent most of his career in Green Bay.

•

14 What NFL team did Tom Landry play for and later help coach as a defensive assistant?

•

15 Who was the first player drafted by the Cowboys and what school did he attend?

•

16 What long-time columnist has covered the Cowboys since their inception and is widely known for "scattershooting"?

•

17 What was the site of the team's first training camp?

•

18 What team did the Cowboys beat to win their first Super Bowl, and who was the game's MVP?

•

19 Match the player with his alma mater:

Rayfield Wright	Elizabeth City
Bob Hayes	Fort Valley State
Jethro Pugh	Florida A&M
Issiac Holt	Alcorn State

•

20 Name the son of a long-time NFL coach who was a Cowboy assistant from 1989 to 1990.

•

21 Name the former Cowboy receiver and the title of his scathing novel about pro football.

•

22 True or false: Roger Staubach holds the team record for career touchdowns.

•

23 Who was a long-time starter at defensive end drafted from the University of Hawaii in 1968?

•

24 What Cowboy offensive lineman had a brother who started at defensive tackle for the Washington Redskins in the 1970s?

•

25 Roger Staubach was one of three quarterbacks drafted by the team in 1964. Name the other two.

•

26 What player won the 1990 Outland Award as the nation's best defensive player?

•

27 Who is the only player in team history with a defensive touchdown in back-to-back games?

•

28 Who tackled Walt Garrison at the goal line in 1973 in one of the most famous plays in *Monday Night Football* history?

•

29 Who once served as a spokesman for the Austin Police Department trying to educate youngsters about the danger of joining gangs?

•

30 Name the current Cowboy assistant who tried unsuccessfully to convince Emmitt Smith to attend the University of Miami.

•

31 What fearsome special teams captain signed as a free agent out of Tennessee in 1983?

•

32 Who once called Tom Landry a "plastic man"?

•

33 What Cowboy quarterback from 1960 to 1963 was known to NFL fans as "The Little General"?

•

34 Everyone knows about Emmitt Smith. How many other Smiths are on the team's all-time roster?

•

35 In what year did the Dallas Cowboys Cheerleaders make their debut?

•

36 Who was the last member of the original Cowboys to retire in 1969?

•

37 Who was the opponent and what was the final outcome of the Cowboys' first regular-season game?

•

38 Name the Cowboys' first 1,000-yard running back.

•

39 Who gave Pete Rozelle his first job in the National Football League?

•

40 In what round of the draft was Roger Staubach selected?

•

41 What Cowboy linebacker can trace his fighting spirit to his father, a former heavyweight boxer?

•

42 Who did the Cowboys select with their first No. 1 selection in the entire NFL draft in 1974?

•

43 What world-class sprinter from the University of Oregon is the team's all-time interception leader, with 52?

•

44 Who holds the team record for touchdown catches?

•

45 Who anchored the Cowboys' Doomsday Defense as a fixture at middle linebacker for fourteen years?

•

46 Name the only Cowboy ever to graduate from Amherst.

•

47 Who was the opponent for the Cowboys' first game at Texas Stadium?

•

48 Name the former St. Louis Cardinal who had one of the most famous drops in Super Bowl history while playing for the Cowboys.

•

49 Who kicked the longest punt in team history?

•

50 Whose brother was a Hall of Fame college and pro basketball player?

COWBOYS IN ARMS

Right from the start, the Dallas Cowboys began building their football team with a heavy emphasis on the quarterback position.

And while the men who lined up over center for the franchise came in a variety of sizes, shapes, and temperaments, there's little question that a major part of the Cowboys' success over the seasons has been directly attributable to each man's ability to execute the complicated offensive formations drawn up for twenty-nine years by Tom Landry and in the last four by Jimmy Johnson.

The smallest man came first. Though Eddie LeBaron stood only five feet seven inches, the Cowboys sent a first- and sixth-round draft choice to the Washington Redskins to acquire the Little General's services in 1960, their first year in the league. LeBaron had been a starter in Washington since 1952, and Landry decided he needed a fully experienced man at the position while rookie Don Meredith learned the system.

LeBaron took his lumps those first three years and the Cowboys managed only nine victories over that span, including a winless first season. In 1960, Landry even went to a shuttle quarterback system with LeBaron, Meredith, and Don Heinreich, all to no avail.

Meredith, a hometown hero who had starred at SMU, split the duties with LeBaron in 1961 and 1962 before taking over for good in the 1963 season. And the man who would go on to greater fame as an announcer for ABC's *Monday Night Football* turned the offense into an aerial show through the rest of the 1960s.

In 1964, the Cowboys also took a calculated risk by drafting

Don Meredith *(The Washington Post)*.

Heisman Trophy winner Roger Staubach of Navy in the tenth round, despite his four-year commitment to serve in the military. Staubach served in Vietnam but eventually joined the team in 1969 and split time with Craig Morton.

Staubach finally won the position for good in his third year, and the Cowboys were never the same thereafter. Over the next six seasons, Dallas advanced to the Super Bowl three times, winning in 1977 against a Denver team ironically directed by Morton, who'd been traded west in 1974.

Staubach was best known for his late-game heroics. Though Landry always called the plays, Staubach, the consummate competitor, executed flawlessly, particularly in the two-minute drill when his team just had to score. Unlike Meredith, the party animal, Captain Comeback was a clean-living family man whose red, white, and blue background helped develop the Cowboys' image as America's Team.

Having sustained one too many concussions, Staubach retired from football after the 1979 season, despite leading the league in passing that year. When he became eligible for the Hall of Fame, he was elected on the first ballot in 1985.

Staubach's successor had a tough act to follow. And while Danny White was a talented athlete, he could never get the team past the NFC title game into a Super Bowl. He retired after the 1988 season, just as the Cowboys were making young Troy Aikman their first-round pick in the 1989 draft.

That was the beginning of a new era for the Cowboys, with Jerry Jones and Jimmy Johnson taking control of the franchise. That first year, Aikman took shot after devastating shot in a 1-15 season, including one game against the Eagles when he was sacked 11 times and humiliated by a Philadelphia defense that taunted him all day.

Three years later came sweet vindication, as Aikman, a six-foot-four 225-pounder, stood his ground and led the Cowboys to their best regular season record of 13-3 and a stunningly easy 55–17 victory over the Buffalo Bills in Super Bowl XXVII. Aikman was named MVP in that game, and at the age of twenty-six has a glorious future with the youngest team in the National Football League.

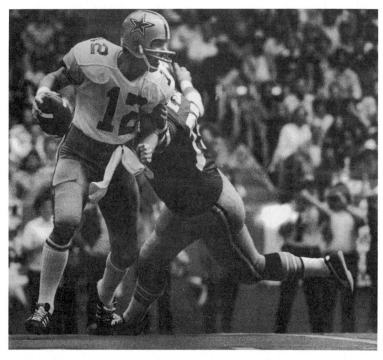

Roger Staubach scrambling away from a tackler (Richard Darcey, *The Washington Post*).

Troy Aikman.

WARM-UP ANSWERS

1 University of Arkansas in 1964.

2 Roger the Dodger, Captain Comeback.

3 Joe Theismann.

4 Thomas Henderson.

5 Calvin Hill, father of Grant Hill of Duke.

6 Ernie Stautner.

7 Clint Longley.

8 Alexander Wright, 102 yards against the Atlanta Falcons on December 22, 1991.

9 Randy White.

10 Defensive end Chad Hennings.

11 Henryetta High School.

12 Bedford Wynne.

13 Bob Lilly, Roger Staubach, Tex Schramm, Tom Landry. Herb Adderly spent most of his career in Green Bay and played for Dallas from 1970 to 1972.

14 New York Giants.

15 Bob Lilly from Texas Christian.

16 Blackie Sherrod.

17 Pacific University in Forest Grove, Oregon.

18 The Cowboys beat the Miami Dolphins, 24–3, in Super Bowl VI. Roger Staubach was MVP.

19 Rayfield Wright, Fort Valley State; Bob Hayes, Florida A&M; Jethro Pugh, Elizabeth City; and Issiac Holt, Alcorn State.

20 David Shula.

21 Peter Gent, *North Dallas Forty.*

22 False. Danny White had 155, Roger Staubach 153.

23 Larry Cole.

24 Cowboy Don Talbert and Redskin Diron Talbert.

25 Billy Lothridge of Georgia Tech and Jerry Rhome of Tulsa.

26 Russell Maryland.

27 Ray Horton against the Giants and Packers in 1991.

28 Redskin safety Ken Houston.

29 Tony Casillas.

30 Running back coach Joe Brodsky.

31 Bill Bates.

32 Duane Thomas.

33 Eddie LeBaron.

34 There are ten other Smiths: Daryle, Donald, J.D., Jackie, Jim Ray, Sean, Timmy, Tody, Vinson, and Waddell.

35 1972.

36 Don Meredith.

37 Dallas lost to the Pittsburgh Steelers, 35–28, on September 24, 1960.

38 Calvin Hill with 1,036 yards in 1972.

39 Tex Schramm.

40 Tenth round in 1964.

41 Ken Norton, Jr.

42 Ed "Too Tall" Jones.

43 Mel Renfro.

44 Bob Hayes with 71.

45 Lee Roy Jordan.

46 Jean Fugett.

47 The New England Patriots, who lost, 44–21, on October 24, 1971.

48 Jackie Smith dropped a pass in the end zone in Super Bowl XIII against the Pittsburgh Steelers, who won, 35–31.

49 Ron Widby, 84 yards against the New Orleans Saints, November 3, 1968.

50 Offensive tackle Bruce Walton, brother of Bill Walton.

FIRST AND TEN

1   What starting linebacker spent his first two seasons with the team as a defensive lineman?

•

2   The father of what offensive lineman was a high school teammate of Hall of Fame receiver Fred Biletnikoff at Erie (Pa.) Tech?

•

3   Name the player who led the team in sacks the most years.

•

4   True or false: Emmitt Smith was the Cowboys' most prolific all-time rusher.

•

5   Name the team's leading receiver and his total catches in 1960, the first year of the franchise.

•

6   What pigeon-toed receiver still leads the team in total receptions?

•

7   What defensive starter was the Cowboys' last pick in the 1992 draft?

•

8   What team once drafted former Cowboy assistant Dave Wannstedt in the fifteenth round?

•

9   At what school did Jimmy Johnson begin his coaching career?

•

10   Jay Novacek in 1992 matched this former Cowboy as the

only player in team history with 50 or more catches in three straight seasons.

•

11   Before Emmitt Smith did it, who was the last back to lead the NFL in rushing in back-to-back seasons?

•

12   What player did the Cowboys acquire from the Los Angeles Raiders for a fourth-round draft choice in 1991?

•

13   Name the only two rookie quarterbacks who ever started a season opener.

•

14   Rap singer Hammer was a high school teammate of what Cowboy defensive back?

•

15   What 1985 Outland Trophy winner set a school record with 21 tackles behind the line of scrimmage his senior season in college?

•

16   Name the third Cowboy ever drafted from this tiny Georgia school, but only the first to make the team.

•

17   Who were the only NFL running backs ahead of Tony Dorsett when he went over the 12,000-yard mark in 1987?

•

18   Name the only other man besides Tom Landry to coach an NFL team for twenty-nine straight seasons.

•

19   Who were the other inductees in Roger Staubach's 1985 enshrinement into the Pro Football Hall of Fame?

•

20   In what year did the Cowboys begin training camp at California Lutheran in Thousand Oaks?

•

21   Whom did the Cowboys defeat when they won their first NFC championship?

•

22   What long-time Cowboy-hating coach used the slogan "The future is now"?

23 Name the player who was a three-year starter at right tackle from 1987 to 1989 until he switched to guard in 1991.

24 Name the offensive lineman acquired from the Los Angeles Raiders for a fifth-round pick in the 1990 draft.

25 Who once set the Florida state record by high-jumping seven feet, one inch?

26 Who won the NFL's fastest man competition in 1991?

27 Name the Brooklyn-born lineman who began his career with the Green Bay Packers, where he earned a starting spot in 1986 after signing as a free agent.

28 Name the player who led the team in scoring a record nine seasons.

29 What all-pro defensive back led the team in kickoff returns in 1971–72?

30 Built low to the ground, he led the Cowboys in rushing only once, in 1975.

31 Name the three starters on the 1972 Redskins NFC championship team who began their careers as Cowboys in the 1960s.

32 What former Cowboy running back has been the head coach of two NFL teams?

33 What was the nickname of Lance Alworth, who played two seasons for the Cowboys?

34 Name the son of this LSU All-American who had a promising Cowboy career cut short by injury.

35 What former Cowboy linebacker from Boston College went on to start at the same position for the New York Giants?

•

36 Who was Tony Dorsett's coach at the University of Pittsburgh?

•

37 "A pinch between your cheek and gum" was his post-football slogan.

•

38 Name the college basketball star at Utah State who was one of the first free agents to make an impact with the early Cowboys.

•

39 What defensive lineman acquired from the Redskins in 1989 was known as "The Tasmanian Devil"?

•

40 Match the school with the Harris:

Cliff Harris	Oklahoma
Duriel Harris	Ouachita
Rod Harris	New Mexico State
Jim Harris	Texas A&M

•

41 Name nine of the Cowboys' first ten draft choices in 1987 who eventually made the team.

•

42 What fierce blocker was drafted in the second round in 1989 with a choice acquired from the Los Angeles Raiders?

•

43 What 1988 draft choice spent the the 1992 season as a backup to Dan Marino on the Miami Dolphins?

•

44 Pick the team's all-time leader in pass completion percentage.
   a) Danny White
   b) Roger Staubach
   c) Don Meredith
   d) Troy Aikman

•

45 True or false: Bob Hayes had the most seasons leading the team in pass receiving yardage.

•

46 Name the Dallas sportswriter who was the first editor of *The Dallas Cowboys Weekly.*

•

47 What long-time Cowboy equipment manager celebrates his twentieth season with the team in 1993?

•

48 What are the official team colors of the Dallas Cowboys?

•

49 Name the veteran public address voice of Texas Stadium.

•

50 The Cowboys own the record for number of consecutive winning seasons. How many?

TEX AND TOM

For twenty-nine years, Tex Schramm and Tom Landry ran the Dallas Cowboys, taking a lowly expansion franchise in 1960 and developing it into America's Team, one of the most successful organizations in the history of professional sports.

Schramm came first on the recommendation of George Halas of the Chicago Bears. The team's first owner, Clint Murchison, had asked Halas for some possible candidates, and Schramm, a former general manager of the Los Angeles Rams, seemed ideal. Though he was working at the time as an assistant director of programming for CBS Sports, Schramm had the perfect pedigree—a degree in journalism from the University of Texas and the best first name an owner could ask for in starting up a team in the Lone Star State.

Schramm was hired, and immediately set about rounding up players. He paid his old team, the Rams, $5,000 for scouting reports on free agents who might be available to supplement the talent—or lack of talent—he'd get in the expansion pool and the college draft. He also convinced Don Meredith, the hero of the hometown Southern Methodist University team, not to play in the American Football League, giving him a lucrative guaranteed contract.

But Schramm's best acquisition would come when he decided to offer the head coaching job to a promising young assistant coach on the New York Giants. Landry signed up for five years at the salary of $34,500 a year and also got from Schramm a pledge that he would have complete autonomy in the football decisions, while Schramm would run the organization.

For the next twenty-nine years, that's exactly how it worked. Landry's teams struggled at first, but eventually

Tom Landry.

Tex Schramm.

flourished in the 1970s with an innovative and highly complex offense and the flex defense he'd been using since his days with the Giants. The end result was five Super Bowl appearances, two championships, an overall record of 270-178-6, and enshrinement in the Pro Football Hall of Fame in 1990.

Schramm became the guiding force of the Cowboys and one of the most powerful men in the NFL. He was chairman of the league's competition committee, the panel responsible for determining the way the game is played, and put together an organization in Dallas that was a model for success.

Under Schramm and Landry, the Cowboys had twenty straight winning seasons. Texas Stadium and the game's first luxury boxes were Schramm's idea. So were the Dallas Cowboys Cheerleaders, the *Dallas Cowboys Weekly* newspaper, and the team's current state-of-the-art training headquarters at Valley Ranch in the Dallas suburbs.

When Jerry Jones bought the team in 1989 and fired Schramm and Landry, there was a public outcry at the tackiness of it—all aimed at the brash Arkansas oilman who had perpetrated the dirty deed. Still, some former Cowboys shed few tears for two men who also were often perceived as cold, calculating, and occasionally cruel in their handling of human relations and contract negotiations.

Schramm and Landry both still live in Dallas. Schramm is retired and spends a good deal of his time fishing in Florida. Landry is still a popular motivational speaker and works diligently for the Fellowship of Christian Athletes. Neither man has been inducted into the team's Ring of Honor in Texas Stadium honoring the greats in Cowboy history, a source of some controversy in the past. Jerry Jones says he'd like to have both of them in the Ring, and Schramm says he'd be willing if Landry would go with him. Claiming schedule conflicts prevented him from attending previous ceremonies, Landry finally agreed to be honored and Schramm is certain to follow.

Their names obviously belong alongside those of Roger Staubach, Bob Lilly, and Tony Dorsett at Texas Stadium. Their contributions to the team, the town, and the National Football League may never be duplicated and will never be forgotten.

FIRST AND TEN
ANSWERS

1 Vinson Smith.

2 Mark Stepnoski, son of Marty.

3 Harvey Martin, seven years (1974–77, 1979–80, 1982).

4 False. Tony Dorsett had 12,036 yards; Emmitt Smith had 4,213.

5 Jim Doran, 31 catches for 554 yards.

6 Drew Pearson with 489.

7 Cornerback Larry Brown.

8 Green Bay Packers.

9 Defensive line coach at Louisiana Tech in 1965.

10 Herschel Walker.

11 Eric Dickerson of the Los Angeles Rams in 1983–84.

12 Quarterback Steve Beuerlein.

13 Roger Staubach and Troy Aikman.

14 Vince Albritton.

15 Tony Casillas at Oklahoma.

16 Defensive back Kenneth Gant of Albany State.

17 Walter Payton, Jim Brown, Franco Harris.

18 Curly Lambeau of the Green Bay Packers from 1921 to 1949.

19 Pete Rozelle, Joe Namath, O. J. Simpson, and Frank Gatski.

20 1963.

21 San Francisco lost, 17–10, in 1970.

22 George Allen of the Washington Redskins.

23 Kevin Gogan.

24 John Gesek.

25 Receiver Alvin Harper.

26 Alexander Wright.

27 Alan Veingrad.

28 Kicker Rafael Septien from 1978 to 1986.

29 Cliff Harris.

30 Robert Newhouse.

31 Ray Schoenke, John Wilbur, Brig Owens.

32 Dan Reeves, Denver Broncos and New York Giants.

33 Bambi.

34 Billy Cannon, Jr.

35 Steve DeOssie.

36 Johnny Majors.

37 Walt Garrison.

38 Cornell Green.

39 Dean Hamel.

40 Cliff Harris, Ouachita; Duriel Harris, New Mexico State; Rod Harris, Texas A&M; and Jim Harris, Oklahoma.

41 1. DT Danny Noonan; 2. CB Ron Francis; 3. OL Jeff Zimmerman; 4. WR Kelvin Martin; 5. WR Everett Gay; 7. QB Kevin Sweeney; 8. RB Alvin Blount; 9. LB Dale Jones.

42 Fullback Daryl Johnston.

43 Scott Secules of Virginia.

44 a) Troy Aikman, 60.21 percent.

45 False. Tony Hill led the team eight times, Bob Hayes five times.

46 Steve Perkins.

47 William T. "Buck" Buchanan.

48 Royal blue, metallic silver blue, and white.

49 Murphy Martin.

50 Twenty seasons.

SECOND AND FIVE

1   Who bought the team from Clint Murchison in 1984 and sold it to Jerry Jones in 1989?

•

2   Who caught the Hail Mary pass that beat the Minnesota Vikings in the first round of the 1975 play-offs?

•

3   Name the year and the opponent for the team's first sellout.

•

4   Name the Baltimore Colt kicker who beat the Cowboys with a late field goal in Super Bowl III.

•

5   Whom did the Cowboys beat for Jimmy Johnson's first NFL head coaching victory?

•

6   What did the Cowboys receive in the 1989 trade of Herschel Walker to the Minnesota Vikings?

•

7   In 1989, who was the first Cowboy inducted into the team's Ring of Honor at Texas Stadium since Roger Staubach in 1983?

•

8   How many times have the Cowboys won at least 11 games?

•

9   Who was the Cowboys' opponent the night that produced the largest audience ever to view a game on Turner Network Television?

•

10 What team did the Cowboys beat on January 5, 1992, to post their first play-off road victory since 1980?

•

11 True or false: The Cowboys are the only team in NFL history to have the league's leading rusher and receiver in the same year.

•

12 Jimmy Johnson won only three of seven bowl games as a collegiate coach at Oklahoma State and Miami. Name the bowls and the teams he beat.

•

13 Name the assistant coach who played quarterback at the University of Oregon and was recruited there by former Rams coach John Robinson.

•

14 Who were the three running backs who were No. 1 draft choices coached by assistant Joe Brodsky at Miami?

•

15 Who was the Minnesota Vikings' second-round choice in 1985 and led his team in interceptions a year later?

•

16 Who was the first Cowboy wide receiver to play in the Pro Bowl since Drew Pearson in 1977?

•

17 Who was the oldest player on the team's active roster in Super Bowl XXVII?

•

18 Who graduated first in his high school class in upstate New York?

•

19 Name the player who will go down in history for one of the most famous fumbles in the Super Bowl.

•

20 Who was the big playmaker on the '92 Cowboys who finished among the nation's top ten punt returners in each of his last three years at Boston College?

•

21 Russell Maryland was one of only five defensive tackles selected with the first choice in the NFL draft. Name the other four.

•

22   Who is the talkative tackle who went on a diet and helped shape up the team's offensive line in 1992?

•

23   Who holds the team record for best average punt return yardage:
   a) Kelvin Martin
   b) Butch Johnson
   c) Mel Renfro
   d) Bob Hayes

•

24   True or false: Tony Dorsett is the Cowboys' all-time leading scorer.

•

25   Who was the Cowboys' leading rusher in their first season?

•

26   What small Oklahoma school did Thomas "Hollywood" Henderson attend?

•

27   What former head coach at Marshall University and the University of Virginia spent the 1968 season as a wide receiver with the Cowboys?

•

28   What wide receiver from the University of Tennessee also was a world-class hurdler?

•

29   What player came to the Cowboys from Vienna, Austria, and never played college football?

•

30   Who came home to play in Dallas in 1971 after a brilliant career in Green Bay?

•

31   What 1988 eighth-round draft choice eventually became a starting running back for the Miami Dolphins in 1992?

•

32 What tight end made the Pro Bowl in 1961, his only season with the Cowboys?

•

33 Name the only three players on the 1992 team who have played in the NFL for ten years or longer.

•

34 Who are the four starters taken in the first four rounds of the 1989 draft?

•

35 What versatile veteran offensive lineman has played both offense and defense in Dallas and once had six tackles in 1986 playing for injured Randy White?

•

36 What assistant coach once played for fellow staff member Joe Brodsky on Miami's Jackson High School team?

•

37 Who was known as "Mr. Cowboy"?

•

38 Who was known for singing "Turn Out the Lights" on national TV?

•

39 What massive offensive tackle cost the Cowboys a No. 1, 2, and two No. 5 choices in the 1967 draft?

•

40 Name the opponent that inflicted the worst loss in team history.

•

41 Don Meredith once passed for 460 yards in a single game. Who was the opponent?

•

42 What West Virginian holds the team record for longest fumble return?

•

43 Name the co-MVPs in Super Bowl XII in New Orleans.

•

44 What was the Cowboys' record in 1984 when their streak of eight straight play-off appearances ended?

•

45 Who was the opponent for the Cowboys' first NFL victory?

•

46 What's the nickname of Cowboy cornerback Kevin Smith?

•

47 What team employed defensive assistant Jim Eddy as defensive coordinator in 1992?

•

48 Before linebacker Robert Jones broke the team rookie record for tackles with 108 in 1992, who held the old mark?

•

49 True or false: Emmitt Smith was the first NFL rushing champion to play in a Super Bowl.

•

50 Name the new defensive coordinator for the Denver Broncos who was a star defensive back for the Cowboys in the 1970s.

EMMITT THE GREAT

For most of his young life, running with the football has seemed so carefree and easy, so natural for Emmitt Smith, the NFL's leading rusher in 1991 and 1992 and a three-year veteran who only turned twenty-five in May of 1993 and answers to the nicknames "Magic Man" or "Magician." Defensive back Issiac Holt will often ask Smith before games, "Magic, are you going to disappear on someone today?"

In 1992, Smith gained a team record 1,713 yards on 373 carries, set another record with 18 touchdowns, and is already fifth on the team's all-time rushing list after only three seasons. Dallas is 29-1 when he carries 20 or more times, 21-1 when he rushes for 100 or more yards, and has won 17 straight games in which Smith rushed for 100 or more yards.

For Smith, a compact five-foot-nine, 209-pound native of Pensacola, Florida, with redwood thighs and a rippled upper body, it's been like that since he started playing football as an eight-year-old. Said Cowboys running back coach Joe Brodsky, "No one has ever been able to stop him, at any level."

At Escambia High School, where Smith was a starter as a freshman, he gained 8,804 career yards, scored 106 touchdowns, and was named *Parade* magazine's national player of the year. At the University of Florida, he established 58 school records and became only the second freshman to finish in the top ten in Heisman Trophy balloting. He reached 1,000 yards rushing in his seventh game that season, faster than any other freshman in history.

Smith ran for 100 yards in 70 of his 83 high school and college games. Yet, when he decided to leave school after his junior year at Florida, Smith wasn't the first back taken in the

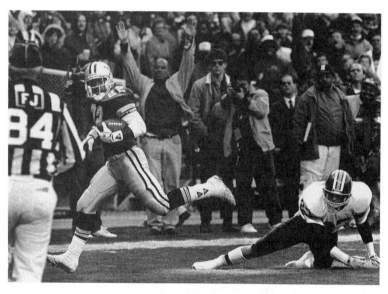

Emmitt Smith scores another touchdown (Rich Lipski, *The Washington Post*).

1990 draft. That distinction went to Blair Thomas, selected by the New York Jets. As the first round wore on and Smith remained on the board, the incredulous Cowboys traded their own first pick and a third-round choice to the Steelers for the chance to make him the seventeenth selection.

How could sixteen teams have passed on Emmitt Smith?

"Speed," said Brodsky, mindful of the 4.55 clocking for forty yards attributed to Smith in most scouting reports. "Had to be, unless people were just plain stupid. He doesn't show the burst you want to see from an average-sized back. But I've never seen Emmitt caught from behind, not in high school, not in college, not up here."

Smith is still slightly perturbed about his college career, especially about falling off most Heisman Trophy lists by his junior year.

"Personally, I don't feel like I got the credit I deserved," he said. "I did some things at the University of Florida under adverse conditions. We had no depth because the probation took away scholarships. The coach [Galen Hall] resigned, it was like a scandal a day. I guess when people thought about Florida, they thought probation. They put me in that same category as all that stuff, like a delinquent, something society didn't need.

"But I'm not out to prove to the world that they made a mistake. In the NFL, they look at you like a prototype. They want a guy who runs 4.3 and bench-presses 350 to 400 pounds, who stands six-one and weighs 215 and has the hands of Michael Irvin [his best friend] and the speed of Barry Sanders. Then along comes myself and they don't know what to do.

"Nobody knows how fast I can run because I'm only giving them what I want them to see. I don't know what I do or why I do it. I believe I could probably run a 4.37 or a 4.39 if I had to. In this league, you have to have all the moves. I have enough speed, I have elusiveness, and I have balance. When I'm running, I know what I'm doing. Running the ball is like an art, you've got to create new and different tactics to get around a guy. Some people know you're coming, but they still can't do anything about it."

Smith said all of that smiling broadly. Brodsky said he's shy and somewhat introverted, "a genuinely nice kid" who's still slightly uncomfortable with his superstar status and its trappings. There are lots of trappings. He's got a Mercedes in the parking lot. He wears a diamond in one ear, a couple of gold chains around his neck, and a gold watch mere mortals might have difficulty lifting off the bedroom dresser. In the summer of '93, Smith was also involved in a protracted and occasionally nasty contract holdout, another sure sign of his ascension to the league's elite franchise player category.

Despite his size, he's incredibly durable. And despite all the wicked hits he takes game after game, he hasn't missed a start in three years, and his streak of 52 starts is a team high.

"You love to block for the guy," said fullback Daryl Johnston. "He seems to do something different every week. He has a knack for hitting a hole at the right time; sometimes it's a quick move, sometimes he'll cut back. Every game you see one move that's better than the last time."

Brodsky said the Cowboys would like to rest Smith more every now and then, use backups to get him out for a series or two. Yet, there have been times when Brodsky thought Smith was catching his breath on the bench, only to turn back toward the field and see Smith in the huddle.

"He sneaks in there," Brodsky said. "He loves to play."

SECOND AND FIVE
ANSWERS

1 H. R. "Bum" Bright.

2 Drew Pearson, 50 yards from Roger Staubach.

3 In 1965, a crowd of 76,251 watched the Cleveland Browns beat the Cowboys, 24–17, at the Cotton Bowl.

4 Jim O'Brien.

5 The Washington Redskins in 1989.

6 Five players, six conditional draft choices, and a 1992 draft choice.

7 Lee Roy Jordan.

8 Twelve.

9 Phoenix, a 17–9 loser that Sunday night, Sept. 27, 1991.

10 The Chicago Bears.

11 True. Emmitt Smith and Michael Irvin in 1991.

12 1983 Bluebonnet Bowl (Baylor, 24–14); 1987 Orange Bowl (Oklahoma, 20–14); 1988 Orange Bowl (Nebraska, 23–3).

13 Offensive coordinator Norv Turner.

14 Ottis Anderson, Alonzo Highsmith, and Cleveland Gary.

15 Cornerback Issiac Holt.

16 Michael Irvin in 1991.

17 Jim Jeffcoat, thirty-two years old.

18 Daryl Johnston.

19 Leon Lett in Super Bowl XXVII against Buffalo in 1993.

20 Kelvin Martin.

21 Buck Buchanan (1963), Bubba Smith (1967), Ken Sims (1982), Steve Entmann (1992).

22 Nate Newton.

23 d) Bob Hayes, 11.1 yards.

24 False. Rafael Septien with 874 points. Dorsett is second with 516.

25 L. G. Dupre with 362 yards in 104 attempts.

26 Langston University.

27 Sonny Randle.

28 Richmond Flowers.

29 Kicker Toni Fritsch.

30 Forrest Gregg.

31 Mark Higgs.

32 Dick Bielski.

33 Bill Bates, Jim Jeffcoat, and Mark Tuinei.

34 Troy Aikman, Daryl Johnston, Mark Stepnoski, Tony Tolbert.

35 Mark Tuinei.

36 Special teams coach Joe Avezzano.

37 Bob Lilly, who never missed a game in fourteen years with the team.

38 Don Meredith.

39 Ralph Neely.

40 The Chicago Bears beat the Cowboys 44–0 in 1985.

41 San Francisco in 1963.

42 Chuck Howley, 97 yards against Atlanta in 1966.

43 Randy White and Harvey Martin.

44 The Cowboys finished 8–6.

45 Dallas scored 10 points in the final 56 seconds to beat the Pittsburgh Steelers, 27–24, in the 1961 season opener.

46 Pup.

47 Houston Oilers.

48 Eugene Lockhart, 86 in 1984.

49 True.

50 Charlie Waters.

INTERMISSION

THE BRAIN TRUST:
JERRY AND JIMMY

Not long after Judge Clarence Thomas was confirmed as the newest member of the Supreme Court, he accompanied Dallas Cowboys owner Jerry Jones to RFK Stadium to watch their favorite football team play the Washington Redskins. Naturally, Redskins owner Jack Kent Cooke wanted to meet them both, and invited them to stop by his private box before the game to say hello.

"That was my first time meeting Mr. Cooke," Jones said, "and we had a nice little visit before the game. After a while, I said to him, 'Mr. Cooke, I've got to go down and tell Jimmy Johnson what plays to call in the fourth quarter.' He looked at me like I was crazy, and then he said, 'Why Jerry, that's just obscene.' "

Jones was having a little fun with the Redskins' owner that afternoon, though Cooke's jesting comment was probably not that far off target from a view held by some of Jones's fellow owners. In the clubby, stiff-upper-lip boardrooms around the National Football League, where owners are seldom seen or heard, Jones's brash, out-front, it's-my-team-and-I'll-do-what-I-want-to style not only goes against the grain, it's like a fingernail across the blackboard.

If you think fifty-year-old Arkansas-bred Jerry Jones cares much about what his fat cat fraternity brothers might think of one of the newest pledges to the club, think again. Truth is, Jerry Jones has become one of the biggest stars of his own show, a man who's never turned down an interview in his life.

At Super Bowl XXVII, the NFL even assigned him his own table during interview sessions normally reserved for players and coaches. And almost every day that week, writers were three-deep around him as he talked about the satisfaction the

Cowboys owner Jerry Jones (Dallas Cowboys).

1992 season and his team had provided for him and his old college football teammate, Cowboy head coach Jimmy Johnson.

He loves talking about his team—"I have my knee pads on wanting people to be interested in the Dallas Cowboys," he says—and is easily the most accessible owner in the NFL, not only to the media but to the Cowboys' reborn-again legion of fans back home and all around the country.

He's got his own television show, his own radio show, his own weekly press luncheon, and his own column in *The Dallas Morning News* the day after every game. But most of all, he's got himself a football team for the nineties, four years after he had a football team not fit for public display.

"The word *vindication* is not there for me," Jones said. "But this shouldn't really surprise anyone. If anyone is willing to take a big risk, do his homework, and ask the right questions, you can be a success in anything you do. Most of us don't have that luxury. I'm fortunate, I did."

It was not that way in the beginning. Jones had played on the 1964 University of Arkansas national championship team with Johnson and made his fortune in the risk-it-all oil and gas exploration business. But when he bought the team for $150 million, he was immediately vilified, yes, even mocked as an Arkansas hillbilly who had just done the unthinkable, firing iconlike Tom Landry even before the ink was dry on his purchase agreement and hiring his old pal, Jimmy Johnson, away from the University of Miami.

Jones said he clearly did not handle the Landry firing very well, though there was no doubt in his mind a change had to be made. He also got plenty of hate mail not long after, equally balanced by messages of support and strong votes of confidence from a number of former Cowboy players, including Roger Staubach and Bob Lilly, Hall of Famers both.

"We had thousands of letters," Jones said, "and about half of it was positive. The other half was negative in various degrees. But there is a misnomer that there was no support there. That's wrong. People did understand you have to be decisive and make hard decisions."

He says now neither he nor Johnson wavered in their plans,

even during that 1-15 first-year disaster when the Cowboys' Valley Ranch complex was equipped with a revolving front door and no source of talent—trades, Plan B moves, claims off the waiver wire—went untapped. Trading veterans for draft choices, including the controversial Herschel Walker deal, eventually turned the franchise around, but Jones will admit now there was some hesitation on pulling the trigger to trade away the team's most valuable player in the prime of his career.

"Most of my life I've dealt with risk-reward situation decision-making," said Jones. "If you get to this position, you do the same thing. I thought if we could make good things happen, the rewards would justify the risks. We've been willing to take risks from the first day."

It also helped that Jones and Johnson were comfortable with each other, though they are not especially close and more than occasionally clashed on the road to Super Bowl XXVII. Jones is a kissy-huggy family man, and has brought two of his children into the organization. Johnson is a loner, a man who didn't even ask his parents to come to the Super Bowl for fear they'd become a distraction.

Johnson, a native Texan, has always been known as a brilliant motivator of football players and a superb judge of talent. His philosophy as a head coach at Oklahoma State and the University of Miami, where his team won the national championship in 1987, has been simple enough. "I always look for big playmakers, guys who make things happen," he said. "Chances are if they're making big plays in high school, they'll do it in college, too. If they do it in college, they can do it at this level. I want great athletes, and we always look for speed."

Johnson suffers deeply when the Cowboys lose. After a heartbreaking loss on a last-minute fumble against the Redskins at RFK Stadium in December 1992, Johnson fairly bit off his words as he addressed the media. That night, on the team's charter flight back home, he lost his temper at several players he thought were taking the loss too lightly. And the next day, when he met the Dallas media at his weekly press

Head coach Jimmy Johnson congratulates Steve Beuerlein after a touchdown pass (Rich Lipski, *The Washington Post*).

conference, he was almost in tears as he recounted how upset he'd been by the loss.

"Fundamentally," Jones said of Johnson, "I have great respect for his intellect, great respect for his people skills, his motivational skills. And we share two philosophies. I believe you win with defense. So does he. He also believes in positive reinforcement, and that's the way I've conducted my business affairs all my life."

But now there is only one business affair that dominates his life. Owner Jones also is president and general manager of the Cowboys and has turned over his other affairs to underlings in his company. He says that's why he was so out front during the Super Bowl, as a working executive vitally involved in almost every aspect of his team's operation, "but never between the white lines.

"I think there are just so many different structures in ownership in the NFL and sports," Jones said. "My situation was that I personally put up more money than anyone in the history of sports. I paid a great deal for the Cowboys and the stadium. It was my own money, not a consortium. I did not get a lot of financing. That's a real good way to get committed. The big decision I had to make was that if I made this commitment, will my other business be okay if I run the Cowboys? If you spend one hundred percent of your time on the Cowboys, and I do, then the way we're structured is a good way to do it."

Johnson said he often goes days without meeting with the owner, only because they try to stay out of each other's way. "The thing I try to do is keep him aware of everything we're doing," Johnson said. "The need for us to talk is not as much as it was in the early days. I think it works just fine. We're both looking at the same goal."

Said Jones, "I expect us to be at a competing level from now on. When I bought the Cowboys, it never occurred to me that we wouldn't win football games and would not be competing in play-offs and Super Bowls. It would have been a rough life for me."

And Jimmy Johnson, too.

THIRD AND TWO

1   What All-American end from Rice University played for the Cowboys from 1964 to 1966?

•

2   Name the three Plan B free agents signed in 1990 who started against the Buffalo Bills in the Super Bowl.

•

3   What did the Cowboys get in return when they traded quarterback Steve Walsh to the New Orleans Saints in 1990?

•

4   True or false: The Cowboys played in a sold-out stadium in all 16 regular-season games in 1992.

•

5   Name the only three NFL teams to make the play-offs more seasons than the Cowboys' twenty.

•

6   Name the three teams that beat the Cowboys in 1992.

•

7   In 1992, punter Mike Saxon set a team record with 166 career kicks inside the opponents' 20-yard line. Who held the old record?

•

8   Until Emmitt Smith scored 18 rushing touchdowns in 1992, three players held the team record. Name them.

•

9   Who has the most play-off victories in the history of the NFL?
    a) Dallas Cowboys
    b) Oakland Los Angeles Raiders
    c) Washington Redskins
    d) Los Angeles Rams

10 The Cowboys became the first team to appear in six Super Bowls in 1992. Name the two teams that have been in five.

11 Name the Cowboy on the 1992 team who has played in the most play-off games.

12 Name the player who had the best single-game pass-catching day of the 1992 season.

13 Name the only player on defense who started every game for the Cowboys in 1992.

14 Match the back with his college:

Don Perkins   Yale
Duane Thomas   New Mexico
Calvin Hill   Oklahoma State
Walt Garrison   West Texas State

15 What defensive lineman from the University of Nebraska led the team in sacks in 1988 with 7½?

16 What is Jay Novacek's nickname?

17 What two Cowboy pass-catchers are long-time friends who grew up in Fort Lauderdale, Florida, and were teammates at the University of Miami?

18 Name the seven rookies on the team's 1992 Super Bowl roster.

19 Who was the MVP of Super Bowl V?

20 What was the nickname of the Cowboys' defense in the 1970s?

21 Name the only player ever drafted by the Cowboys from Carson-Newman College.

●

22 True or false: Troy Aikman has the team record for most passing yards in a game.

●

23 Name the player who led the Cowboys in scoring in their first season.

●

24 Against what team did the Cowboys end their ten-game losing streak in 1960?

●

25 Who kicked the field goal that provided the Cowboys' first NFL victory?

●

26 Name the Redskin kicker and native Texan whom Tex Schramm once accused of using an illegal shoe.

●

27 What former Cowboy quarterback led the Denver Broncos against his old teammates in Super Bowl XII?

●

28 Bob Lilly was inducted into the Pro Football Hall of Fame along with this former teammate.

●

29 When Tom Landry won his 200th game in 1980, who were the only two coaches with more victories?

●

30 What was the site and the year of the Cowboys' first game on foreign soil?

●

31 What job did Tex Schramm take when he resigned from the Cowboys?

●

32 Who has the longest punt in Cowboy history?

●

33 What is the largest margin of victory in the team's history?

●

34 What running back led the Cowboys in receiving in 1972–73?

•

35 Name the top four rushers in team history.

•

36 Big brother was Bubba; name the little brother who played for the Cowboys in 1971–72.

•

37 What Washington, D.C. native played for two years with the Cowboys before becoming a star receiver with the Cleveland Browns in the 1970s?

•

38 Acquired from the Pittsburgh Steelers, he was a dangerous third-down back in the 1970s.

•

39 What one-year defensive tackle in 1987 shared the same name as a Hall of Fame baseball pitcher for the Washington Senators?

•

40 Name the current Cowboy defensive back who played running back in high school and linebacker at Arizona State.

•

41 Name the only two freshmen in the history of Heisman Trophy voting to finish in the top ten.

•

42 Name the rookie running back who started the 1979 season opener.

•

43 In college, he won the Western Athletic Conference decathlon championship in 1984.

•

44 Name the player who didn't start football until his junior year of high school and was a star running back at Westchester High in Los Angeles.

•

45 Name the only two rookies since 1965 who started a season opener at wide receiver.

•

46 Who is the team's all-time play-off interception leader?

47 True or false: The Cowboys set a team record for quarterback sacks allowed in 1992.

•

48 Name the player with the longest consecutive-game starting streak.

•

49 What was the site of the smallest crowd in team history?

•

50 Who has the team record for passes intercepted in a single play-off game?

COWBOYS AND
INDIANS: A GRAND
RIVALRY

For most of the last three decades, the Dallas Cowboys' rivalry with the Washington Redskins has been one of the most intense in all of sports. These two teams love to hate each other, and with some good reason.

"The Cowboys had always felt one team in the league they could beat was the Redskins," said Bobby Mitchell, a former running back and wide receiver who is now the Redskins' assistant general manager. "From the day they first came into the league it was like that. I played against them then; I knew how they felt. Most of the time, they were right."

More seeds were planted out west, when the late George Allen was head coach of the Los Angeles Rams. Allen was an unconventional fellow who thought the whole world was out to get him. Because Cowboys president and general manager Tex Schramm and then-Commissioner Pete Rozelle were close friends, Allen thought the two were constantly conspiring.

During the 1967 season, Schramm charged Allen with spying on Cowboy practices the week before the teams were scheduled to play. He'd even written down the license plate of a suspicious car parked near the practice field and later traced its rental to a Rams employee. Allen fired right back, charging that the Rams' coaching staff had spotted a spy with binoculars in a eucalyptus tree outside their practice facility and it looked very much like a Cowboy scout.

When Allen went to Washington to coach the Redskins in

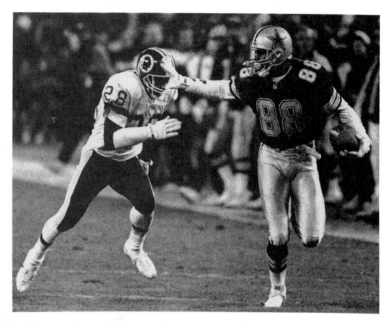

Current star Michael Irvin fends off the Redskins' Darrell Green (Rich Lipski, *The Washington Post*).

1971, he turned up the heat, if only because the Cowboys were now in the same NFC East division and would be challenging the Redskins for the play-offs. Almost every chance he had, Allen would take a poke at the Cowboys. He'd complain about illegal crackback blocks, moan that the league was always on the Cowboys' side, and take sarcastic jabs at Hall of Fame quarterback Roger Staubach. One year, he said the Cowboys used the shotgun offense because Staubach had trouble reading defenses. Another time, he warned that if Staubach scrambled, Allen wouldn't be able to stop his players from knocking his block off.

The Cowboys mostly ignored Allen and his players—the loudest being defensive tackle Diron Talbert, whose brother Don had once played for the Cowboys. But in later years, Tom Landry admitted he had to reassure Staubach that Allen, through Talbert, was only trying to goad him into playing badly.

Schramm did his part to keep up the dialogue. His favorite target was Redskin kicker Mark Moseley, whom he accused of using an illegal kicking shoe. Before one game, Schramm could be seen standing a few feet away from Moseley as the kicker went through his pregame warm-ups, checking to see if the shoe conformed to NFL rules.

In the 1970s, the teams produced some memorable games and plays that will live forever in NFL history. There was Redskin safety Ken Houston tackling Walt Garrison at the goal line to preserve a victory on a Monday night, Cowboy reserve Clint Longley throwing a desperation touchdown pass to Drew Pearson for an unforgettable Thanksgiving Day triumph in 1974, Roger Staubach rallying his team to a 35–34 victory in 1979, eliminating the Redskins from making the play-offs.

It's been that way almost ever since. In the first year of the Jimmy Johnson era, the only team the lowly Cowboys beat in a 1–15 disaster was the Washington Redskins.

In Washington.

Two years later, when the Redskins were riding an 11-game winning streak and dreaming of an undefeated season, the Cowboys came to RFK Stadium and knocked them back to reality. And will anyone ever forget their last meeting in 1992, a game the Cowboys had in their pocket until a controversial fumble—or an incomplete pass, according to any red-blooded Texan—by Troy Aikman was recovered in the end zone by the Redskins for a touchdown and a stunning upset victory?

Though Joe Gibbs is no longer around to match wits with Jimmy Johnson, no one doubts the rivalry will continue well into the 1990s. After all, the Redskins' new head coach, Richie Petitbon, played for George Allen in Chicago, Los Angeles, and Washington and has been the Redskins' defensive coordinator the last ten years. Clearly, this is one rivalry that only gets better as the years wear on.

THIRD AND TWO
ANSWERS

1 Buddy Dial.

2 Tight end Jay Novacek, linebacker Vinson Smith, and safety James Washington.

3 A first- and third-round choice in 1991 and a conditional second-round pick in 1992.

4 True.

5 Los Angeles Rams, Cleveland Browns, and New York Giants, all with 22.

6 Philadelphia Eagles (31–7), Los Angeles Rams (27–23), Washington Redskins (20–17).

7 Danny White, with 159.

8 Tony Dorsett (1977), Herschel Walker (1986), and Emmitt Smith (1991) each scored 12 touchdowns.

9 a) Dallas Cowboys, with 24.

10 Washington Redskins and Miami Dolphins.

11 Charles Haley.

12 Emmitt Smith, with 12 receptions for 67 yards against the Phoenix Cardinals.

13 Tony Tolbert.

14 Don Perkins, New Mexico; Duane Thomas, West Texas State; Calvin Hill, Yale; and Walt Garrison, Oklahoma State.

15 Danny Noonan.

16 Paycheck.

17 Wide receiver Michael Irvin and tight end Alfredo Roberts.

18 Lin Elliott, Chad Hennings, Clayton Holmes, Robert Jones, Jimmy Smith, Kevin Smith, and Darren Woodson.

19 Chuck Howley.

20 The Doomsday Defense.

21 Clayton Holmes.

22 False. Don Meredith has the record, 460 yards against the San Francisco 49ers in 1963.

23 Kicker Fred Cone scored 39 points on six field goals and 21 extra points.

24 New York Giants, a 31–31 tie.

25 Allen Green's 27-yard kick beat the Pittsburgh Steelers in the 1961 season opener.

26 Mark Moseley.

27 Craig Morton.

28 Herb Adderly.

29 George Halas and Curly Lambeau.

30 Wembley Stadium in London, England, in 1966.

31 President of the World League of American Football.

32 Ron Widby, 84 yards in 1968.

33 49 points against the Philadelphia Eagles in 1966.

34 Calvin Hill.

35 Tony Dorsett (12,036 yards), Don Perkins (6,217), Calvin Hill (5,009), Robert Newhouse (4,784).

36 Tody Smith.

37 Reggie Rucker in 1971–72.

38 Preston Pearson.

39 Walter Johnson.

40 Darren Woodson.

41 Herschel Walker at Georgia and Emmitt Smith at Florida.

42 Ron Springs.

43 Jay Novacek.

44 Ken Norton, Jr.

45 Bob Hayes and Michael Irvin.

46 Charlie Waters, with nine play-off interceptions.

47 True. The Cowboys allowed only 23 sacks in 1992. The old record was 30 in 1976 and 1989.

48 Lee Roy Jordan with 154.

49 A crowd of 4,954 watched the Cowboys play the Minnesota Vikings in Sioux Falls, South Dakota, in a 1961 preseason game.

50 Roger Staubach, with four.

FOURTH AND
ONE

1   Name the four kickers the Cowboys have used in the last six years.

•

2   What Cowboy receiver once was married to entertainer Joey Heatherton?

•

3   Name the only three quarterbacks in NFL history with a better completion percentage than Troy Aikman's 60.21 mark.

•

4   What member of the 1992 team led the team in career solo tackles?

•

5   Emmitt Smith became the first Cowboy offensive player to start back-to-back Pro Bowls since these two players on the 1981–82 team.

•

6   Who was the youngest player on the 1992 Cowboys?

•

7   Which two Cowboy defensive backs were teammates at Baylor University?

•

8   Name the opponent and the site of the largest crowd ever to witness a regular-season Cowboy game.

•

9   Name the two first-round picks in the '92 draft who became rookie starters.

•

10   What player holds the team's career record with four blocked punts?

Tony Dorsett hurdles the Raiders' Lester Hayes (Associated Press).

11 What player now on the team was voted the Cleveland Browns' MVP special teamer in 1990?

12 Name the running back who caught three touchdown passes against the Los Angeles Rams in the 1975 NFC Championship game.

13 What long-time Cowboy executive was the team's main talent scout in the Tom Landry era?

14 Name the two players traded to the Houston Oilers in exchange for the draft choices that allowed the Cowboys to select Too Tall Jones and Danny White in 1974.

15 Who scored the winning touchdown that beat the Cowboys in the 1967 NFL Championship game?

16 Name the two players who led the team in receiving for a club record five years each.

17 With 15,501 yards, Tony Dorsett is the team's all-time combined yardage leader. Who is No. 2?

18 Name the two tight ends who combined for 567 catches from 1973 to 1988.

19 Name the Cowboys' four offensive rookies of the year.

20 Name the only player on the 1989 team to make the Pro Bowl.

21 What former Cowboy linebacker was a long-time assistant under Tom Landry?

22 Name the Super Bowl hero running back for another NFC East team who spent the 1990 season on the Cowboys' roster.

23 Who was Thomas Henderson talking about when he said, "He couldn't spell *cat* if you spotted him the c and the a"?

•

24 What former coach of the San Francisco 49ers played safety for the 1962 Cowboys?

•

25 What former Temple running back played for the Cowboys in 1989 and went by the nickname "Boo-Boo"?

•

26 This quotable Cowboy quarterback, drafted out of Indiana University, was a fan favorite in another NFC East city.

•

27 Who scored the first Cowboy touchdown in Super Bowl XXVII?

•

28 Who was the Cowboys' strength and conditioning coach from 1976 to 1989?

•

29 Match the player with his school:

George Andrie	Michigan State
Dave Manders	Marquette
Bob Breunig	Auburn
Dave Edwards	Arizona State

•

30 True or false: Troy Aikman did not have a 300-yard passing day in the 1992 season.

•

31 Name the player who sacked San Francisco quarterback Steve Young three times in the 1992 NFC Championship game.

•

32 His first catch as a Cowboy helped eliminate the Philadelphia Eagles from the 1992 play-offs.

•

33 What running back on the 1967 team still shares the record for play-off scoring in a single season, with 18 points?

•

34 Name the three Cowboys who hold the team record for interceptions in one game.

•

35 Name the five members of the 1992 Cowboys who were teammates at UCLA.

•

36 Mark Stepnoski was only the second center in team history to make the Pro Bowl. Who was the first?

•

37 Robert Jones was the first rookie linebacker to start a season opener since this player did it in 1963.

•

38 His 92 career starts, including the play-offs, are the most on the team's offensive unit.

•

39 Before they played in Super Bowl XXVII, the Cowboys and Buffalo Bills last met in 1984. Name the only two players on the team in '92 who saw action against the Bills in '84.

•

40 What two Cowboys were teammates at the University of Oklahoma in 1984–85?

•

41 What big-time female tennis star is one of the Cowboys' most ardent fans?

•

42 True or false: Roger Staubach holds the team record for most consecutive passes without an interception.

•

43 Who holds the team's rookie record with 12 touchdowns scored:
    a) Calvin Hill
    b) Tony Dorsett
    c) Duane Thomas
    d) Emmitt Smith

•

44 What Texas Tech hero was the second player drafted by the Cowboys but never played for the team?

•

45 The Cowboys traded their first- and second-round draft choices in 1980 to obtain this defensive lineman from the Baltimore Colts.

•

46 Before long-time Cowboy assistant Gene Stallings went to the University of Alabama, what other NFL franchise did he coach?

•

47 What former player's father was a standout receiver with the Cleveland Browns?

•

48 What position did Charlie Waters play at Clemson?

•

49 Name the only player the Cowboys have ever taken from Ouachita.

•

50 Who led the Cowboys in tackles for lost yardage in 1992?

WHEELING AND
DEALING

Since Jimmy Johnson took control of the Cowboys' football operation in 1989, the head coach had pulled the trigger on a total of forty-eight different trades through the 1993 college draft.

That very first trade to move up in the 1990 draft included a second-round and sixth-round choice to the Los Angeles Raiders for a second-round, a third-round, and a fifth-round pick. It also produced starting fullback Daryl Johnston, who was taken from Syracuse with that second-round pick.

Johnson always has used draft day to wheel and deal. In 1990, Johnson moved up again when he traded a first-round pick and a third-round pick to Pittsburgh in order to draft all-world running back Emmitt Smith in the first round. There were three draft-day trades in 1991 and five draft-day trades in 1992, all with the express purpose of stockpiling draft choices for the future and upgrading the roster immediately. And, in 1993, Johnson made a draft-day trade of an undisclosed pick in '94 to New England for backup quarterback Hugh Millen after losing reserve Steve Beuerlein to free agency.

The boldest move of all came on October 12, 1989, when the Cowboys traded what many thought was their most valuable commodity, running back Herschel Walker, to the Minnesota Vikings.

Out of that deal, the Cowboys obtained five veteran Vikings—Jesse Solomon, David Howard, Alex Stewart, Darrin Nelson, and Issiac Holt. They got a first-round draft choice in 1992, conditional first-round draft choices in 1990 and 1991, conditional second-round choices in 1990, 1991, and 1992, and a conditional third-round choice in 1992. One of those first-

Herschel Walker was at the center of the crucial trade with the Minnesota Vikings (Associated Press).

round picks also led to the Cowboys' drafting of Emmitt Smith in 1990 and standout defensive tackle Russell Maryland in 1991.

The Vikings went for the trade because they mistakenly believed they were one great running back away from making the Super Bowl. The Cowboys made the trade to build for the future, and it paid off dramatically with a Super Bowl triumph three years later.

Teams traded with: Los Angeles Raiders 7, New England 7, Denver 3, Detroit 3, Washington 3, Atlanta 2, Cleveland 2, Green Bay 2, Indianapolis 2, Kansas City 2, Minnesota 2, Pittsburgh 2, San Diego 2, San Francisco 2, Miami 1, New York Giants 1, Seattle 1, Phoenix 1, Houston 1, New Orleans 1, Tampa Bay 1.

HOW THE COWBOYS WERE BUILT

From the Draft (25):

1983	Jim Jeffcoat (1st, Arizona St.)
1987	Kelvin Martin (4th, Boston College)
	Kevin Gogan (8th, Washington)
1988	Michael Irvin (1st, Miami)
	Ken Norton (2nd, UCLA)
	Chad Hennings (11th, Air Force)
1989	Troy Aikman (1st, UCLA)
	Daryl Johnston (2nd, Syracuse)
	Mark Stepnoski (3rd, Pittsburgh)
	Tony Tolbert (4th, Texas–El Paso)
1990	Emmitt Smith (1st, Florida)
	Jimmie Jones (3rd, Miami)
	Kenneth Gant (9th, Albany State)
1991	Russell Maryland (1st, Miami)
	Alvin Harper (1st, Tennessee)
	Dixon Edwards (2nd, Michigan State)
	Godfrey Myles (3rd, Florida)
	Erik Williams (3rd, Central State, Ohio)
	# Tony Hill (4th, Tennessee-Chattanooga)
	Leon Lett (7th, Emporia State, Kansas)
	Larry Brown (12th, TCU)
1992	Kevin Smith (1st, Texas A&M)
	Robert Jones (1st, East Carolina)
	Jimmy Smith (2nd, Jackson State)
	Darren Woodson (2nd, Arizona State)
	Clayton Holmes (3rd, Carson-Newman)

Signed as Free Agents (15):

1983	# Bill Bates (Tennessee)
	Mark Tuinei (Hawaii)
1985	Mike Saxon (San Diego State)
1986	Nate Newton (Florida A&M)
1987	Robert Williams (Baylor)
1989	*Ray Horton (Washington)
1990	*Tommie Agee (Auburn)
	*Jay Novacek (Wyoming)
	*Vinson Smith (East Carolina)
	*James Washington (UCLA)
1991	*# Alfredo Roberts (Miami)
	*Alan Veingrad (East Texas State)

HOW THE COWBOYS WERE BUILT *(Continued)*

Signed as Free Agents (15):

1992   *Frank Cornish (UCLA)
              Lin Elliott (Texas Tech)
             #Melvin Evans (Texas Southern)
              Derrick Gainer (Florida A&M)
              Mickey Pruitt (Colorado)
              Derek Tennell (Western Kentucky)

In Trades (7):

1989   Issiac Holt (Alcorn State, from Minnesota in Herschel
              Walker trade)
1990   John Gesék (Cal. St. Sacramento, from L.A. Raiders for
              fifth-round pick in 1991)
              Dale Hellestrae (SMU, from L.A. Raiders for
              seventh-round pick in 1991)
1991   Steve Beuerlein (Notre Dame, from L.A. Raiders for
              fourth-round pick in 1992)
              Tony Casillas (Oklahoma, from Atlanta for second- and
              eighth-round picks in 1992)
1992   Charles Haley (James Madison, from San Francisco for
              undisclosed draft choices)
              Thomas Everett (Baylor, from Pittsburgh for undisclosed
              1993 draft choice)

*Plan B free agent
#Injured Reserve

FOURTH AND ONE
ANSWERS

1 Lin Elliott (1992), Ken Willis (1990–91), Luis Zendejas (1988–89), Roger Ruzek (1987–89).

2 Lance Rentzel.

3 Joe Montana (63.7), Jim Kelly (60.32), Steve Young (60.29).

4 Ray Horton.

5 Pat Donovan and Tony Dorsett.

6 Cornerback Kevin Smith, then twenty-one years old.

7 Thomas Everett and Darren Woodson.

8 A crowd of 91,505 watched the Cowboys play the Los Angeles Raiders at the L.A. Coliseum October 25, 1992.

9 Cornerback Kevin Smith and linebacker Robert Jones.

10 Issiac Holt.

11 Derrick Gainer.

12 Preston Pearson.

13 Gil Brandt.

14 Tody Smith and Billy Parks.

15 Bart Starr.

16 Drew Pearson (1974–78) and Tony Hill (1979–82, '85).

17 Bob Hayes, with 9,104.

18 Billy Joe DuPree (267 catches) and Doug Cosbie (300).

19 Calvin Hill (1969), Duane Thomas (1970), Tony Dorsett (1977), Emmitt Smith (1990).

20 Herschel Walker.

21 Jerry Tubbs.

22 Timmy Smith.

23 Terry Bradshaw.

24 Dick Nolan.

25 Paul Palmer.

26 Babe Laufenberg, drafted by the Redskins.

27 Jay Novacek on a 23-yard pass from Troy Aikman.

28 Bob Ward.

29 George Andrie, Marquette; Dave Manders, Michigan State; Bob Breunig, Arizona State; and Dave Edwards, Auburn.

30 True. His season high was 272 yards against the Los Angeles Rams.

31 Tony Casillas.

32 Tight end Derek Tennell.

33 Craig Baynham.

34 Herb Adderly, Lee Roy Jordan, Dennis Thurman, all with three interceptions.

35 Troy Aikman, Ken Norton, Jr., Derek Tennell, Frank Cornish, James Washington.

36 Dave Manders.

37 Lee Roy Jordan.

38 Nate Newton.

39 Jim Jeffcoat and Mark Tuinei.

40 Troy Aikman and Tony Casillas.

41 Martina Navratilova.

42 False. Don Meredith had 156, Staubach was next with 149.

43 b) Tony Dorsett.

44 E. J. Holub, who went to the American Football League.

45 John Dutton.

46 Phoenix Cardinals.

47 Mike Renfro, son of Ray Renfro.

48 Flanker.

49 Cliff Harris.

50 Jim Jeffcoat.

OT

1   Name the only two Cowboys in team history with a pass reception and a pass interception in the same game.

•

2   Which player is the only man in team history with more than one punt return of 70 yards or more:
a) Bob Hayes
b) Kelvin Martin
c) Mel Renfro
d) Butch Johnson

•

3   Jay Novacek is the second Cowboy to start back-to-back Pro Bowls at tight end since the 1970s. Who was the last man to do it?

•

4   Tight end Derek Tennell has been in the play-offs with four different teams. Name them.

•

5   When Tom Landry coached the defense for the New York Giants in the 1950s, what Hall of Famer coached the offense?

•

6   Name the former Cowboy linebacker who had a standout season for the Minnesota Vikings in 1992 as a Plan B free agent.

•

7   Who was the team's leading receiver in the NFC Championship game against the San Francisco 49ers in 1992:
a) Michael Irvin
b) Kelvin Martin
c) Emmitt Smith
d) Alvin Harper

Hall of Famer Bob Lilly *(The Washington Post)*.

8 Jay Novacek set a Cowboy record for receptions by a tight end with 68 catches in 1992. Who held the previous single-season record?

9 True or false: Michael Irvin is the only Cowboy with 70 or more catches in consecutive seasons.

10 Who holds the team record for consecutive field goals made?
   a) Rafael Septien
   b) Toni Fritsch
   c) Lin Elliott
   d) Roger Ruzek

11 Until Emmitt Smith scored 18 rushing touchdowns in 1992, who held the previous team record?

12 The Cowboys have lost only one game when Emmitt Smith carried the ball 20 or more times. Name the team they lost to.

13 In a 37–3 victory over the Detroit Lions in 1992, for the first time since 1990 Emmitt Smith was not the team's leading rusher. Who was?

14 When the Cowboys beat the Seattle Seahawks, 27–0, in 1992, it marked their first shutout since the 1978 season. Who was the opponent in that 1978 game?

15 True or false: The Cowboys have the best opening-day record in NFL history.

16 Name the six Cowboys who started every game on offense in 1992.

17 Name the only three players in team history with multiple 100-yard games in the play-offs.

18 True or false: The NFC East is the first division ever to win three straight Super Bowls.

•

19 Until Michael Irvin set the record by leading the team in receiving in eight straight games, name the three receivers who shared the old record of six straight games.

•

20 Until the Cowboys beat the Bears in the first round of the 1991 play-offs, they hadn't won a play-off game since 1981. Who was the opponent in the 1981 game?

•

21 Name the six players on the 1992 team drafted on the first round.

•

22 Name the only eleventh- and twelfth-round players on the 1992 team selected by the Cowboys.

•

23 Name the one other active NFL coach with more victories in the 1990s than Jimmy Johnson.

•

24 What position did former Cowboy defensive coordinator Dave Wannstedt play at the University of Pittsburgh:
   a) defensive tackle
   b) middle linebacker
   c) offensive tackle
   d) fullback

•

25 True or false: Mike Saxon holds the team record for consecutive punts without a block.

•

26 Among the three leading yardage passers in NFL history, name the only other quarterback who surpassed 10,000 yards passing faster than Troy Aikman.

•

27 Who holds the team record for catches in a single game:
   a) Michael Irvin
   b) Emmitt Smith
   c) Lance Rentzel
   d) Drew Pearson

28 Until Emmitt Smith accomplished the feat in 1991–92, who was the last NFL player with back-to-back 1,500-yard rushing seasons?

29 True or false: Nate Newton has the most starts of any current Cowboy.

30 Name the only Cowboy ever to lead the NFL in average punt return yardage.

31 What Cowboy scout once coached the Columbia University football team?

32 Name the Cowboys' early AFL Dallas rival, and where did they move in 1962?

33 What Cowboy running back led the team in rushing in 1975 and spent the last years of his career blocking for Tony Dorsett?

34 Name the leading kickoff returner in the team's inaugural 1960 season.

35 Name the only two Cowboys who have ever led the NFL in interceptions.

36 True or false: No Cowboy has ever led the league in pass receptions.

37 Name the only three NFC teams who lead the all-time series record against the Cowboys.

38 Name the only Cowboy player among the first ten draft choices in 1987 who did not make the team.

39 The Cowboys accused this Redskin receiver of illegal crackback blocks during the 1972 season.

40 Name the two Cowboy players who were the first in NFL history to each have a 100-yard run in the same game.

●

41 How did the Cowboys acquire the No. 1 pick that allowed them to select Tony Dorsett in the 1977 draft?

●

42 Name the Cowboy assistant who is the only player in NCAA history to catch two 99-yard touchdown passes at the University of Houston.

●

43 What was Jimmy Johnson's major at the University of Arkansas?

●

44 What year did the Cowboys begin the tradition of playing on Thanksgiving Day?

●

45 Name the only two Cowboy receivers with 50 or more catches in three straight seasons.

●

46 Since 1979, when defensive statistics were first kept, name the only Cowboy to lead the team in tackles for three straight seasons.

●

47 What fabulous defensive lineman hosted his own radio show and once threw flowers he described as a funeral wreath inside the Washington Redskins' locker room?

●

48 What All-American basketball player did the Cowboys draft with the twentieth pick in the 1966 draft?

●

49 What did the Cowboys have to give up to the Atlanta Falcons to obtain Tony Casillas?

●

50 Name the quarterback who beat the Cowboys in the final minute of their first home game in Dallas in 1960.

OT ANSWERS

1 Benny Barnes in 1976 and Alvin Harper in 1992.

2 b) Kelvin Martin.

3 Billy Joe DuPree in 1977–78.

4 Cleveland Browns, Detroit Lions, Minnesota Vikings, Dallas Cowboys.

5 Vince Lombardi.

6 Jack Del Rio.

7 c) Emmitt Smith, with seven catches for 59 yards.

8 Doug Cosbie with 64 catches.

9 True.

10 c) Lin Elliott with 13 in 1992.

11 Dan Reeves, 16 in 1966.

12 The Washington Redskins, in a 20–17 victory at RFK Stadium December 13, 1992.

13 Curvin Richards, who gained 82 yards in 16 carries. Smith had 67 yards in 19 carries.

14 The Cowboys beat the Baltimore Colts, 38–0, in the season opener.

15 True. The Cowboys' opening-day record is 25-7-1.

16 Right guard John Gesek, right tackle Erik Williams, quarterback Troy Aikman, running back Emmitt Smith, tight end Jay Novacek, and fullback Daryl Johnston.

17 Duane Thomas, Tony Dorsett, Emmitt Smith.

18 True. New York Giants in 1990, Washington Redskins in 1991, and Dallas Cowboys in 1992.

19 Lance Rentzel (1968–69), Bob Hayes (1966–67), and Billy Howton (1961–62).

20 Atlanta lost, 30–27.

21 Jim Jeffcoat, Michael Irvin, Troy Aikman, Emmitt Smith, Russell Maryland, and Alvin Harper.

22 Chad Hennings (eleventh round, 1988), Larry Brown (twelfth round, 1992).

23 San Francisco 49er coach George Seifert.

24 c) offensive tackle.

25 False. Danny White has the record of 341; Saxon has 220.

26 John Unitas in 51 games. Aikman reached 10,000 yards passing in 52 games.

27 c) Lance Rentzel, with 13 catches against the Washington Redskins in 1967.

28 Walter Payton (1984–85).

29 False. Jim Jeffcoat has 127, Nate Newton 92.

30 Bob Hayes in 1968.

31 Jim Garrett.

32 Dallas Texans, who moved to Kansas City and became the Chiefs.

33 Robert Newhouse.

34 Tom Frankhauser.

35 Mel Renfro with 10 in 1969, Everson Walls with 11 in 1981, 7 in 1982, and 9 in 1985.

36 True. Michael Irvin finished second in 1991 with 93 catches.

37 Green Bay Packers lead the series 10–6, Los Angeles Rams lead 13–12, and San Francisco 49ers lead 10–9 with one tie.

38 Joe Onosai, an offensive lineman from Hawaii taken in the sixth round.

39 Lance Alworth.

40 Amos Marsh had a 101-yard kickoff return and Mike Gaechter had a 100-yard pass interception against the Philadelphia Eagles in 1962.

41 The Cowboys traded their No. 1 and three No. 2s to the Seattle Seahawks.

42 Tight end coach Robert Ford.

43 Psychology.

44 1966. In their first Thanksgiving Day game, they beat the Cleveland Browns, 26–14.

45 Herschel Walker and Jay Novacek.

46 Bob Breunig from 1979 to 1981.

47 Harvey Martin.

48 Lou Hudson.

49 Second-round and eighth-round draft choices.

50 John Unitas. He completed a 62-yard touchdown pass to Lenny Moore for a 14–10 Baltimore Colt victory on August 19, 1960.

THE LAST WORD

Some final words on Super Bowl XXVII from newspapers around the country:

Richard Justice, *The Washington Post:* Led by their brilliant young quarterback and backed by a defense that forced a record nine turnovers, the Dallas Cowboys finished what a maverick owner and a rookie coach began dreaming about in the spring of 1989, as they crushed the hapless Buffalo Bills, 52–17, to win Super Bowl XXVII in front of 98,374 today at the Rose Bowl.

Cowboys quarterback Troy Aikman was named most valuable player after a near perfect performance that included 22 completions in 30 pass attempts for 273 yards and four touchdowns. But he could have carved the trophy into small pieces and handed one to running back Emmitt Smith for his 108 rushing yards, another to wide receiver Michael Irvin for 114 receiving yards and still another for an offensive line that neutralized end Bruce Smith and the Bills defense.

Dave Anderson, *The New York Times:* Without a crystal ball or tarot cards, the Super Bowl XXVII coaches defined the difference in last night's game two days before that difference developed. "There's only one ball," Marv Levy, the Buffalo Bills' doomsayer had said on Friday when asked what the key to the game would be. "We got to keep it and they got to try and take it away."

But the Bills didn't keep the ball, the Dallas Cowboys took it away. Nine times. Four interceptions. Five lost fumbles. Some bakeries don't sell that many turnovers.

Jim Murray, *Los Angeles Times:* The NFC beat the AFC in the Super Bowl on Sunday.

And a pie is round, and water is wet and ice is slippery and

President Bill Clinton holds up an honorary Cowboys jersey during a ceremony honoring the Super Bowl champions (Associated Press).

roses are red and violets are blue. The Pope is Catholic and there are bear tracks in the woods and the sun sets in the west.

So did the Buffalo Bills. The score is so embarrassing, I don't think I'll mention it to you. . . . All of the suspense went out of the game with the coin flip. Buffalo won that, but it was all downhill from there.

Bill Lyon, *Philadelphia Inquirer:* Troy Aikman got the blame and the lumps when Dallas was starting from ground zero. Last night, while Dallas stood on the mountain top, he accepted the applause.

As a rookie on a 1-15 disaster of a team just three years ago, Aikman was battered and derided. His was a brutal baptism in the NFL. He was Troy The Surfer Boy, and opposing defenses, especially the Eagles, delighted in pouring in on him in a feeding frenzy. In one game alone, the Eagles mercilessly sacked him 11 times, and there was impolite, vocal questioning of his toughness and his skills.

But now, Aikman has his vindication and his vengeance. In Super Bowl XXVII he was right out of the quarterback manual. Poised. Precise. Unwavering. Resourceful.

Michael Wilbon, *The Washington Post:* Sorry, pathetic, hopeless, pitiful, woeful, forlorn, wretched, fraudulent no-account Buffalo Bills. For a post-game meal they should have been fed Kibbles & Bits from a dish on the floor. The Denver Broncos are off the hook; not even they lost three straight Super Bowls. Nobody had done that, until now. You can't believe that any team that professes to be the representative of any conference could come to a championship game and be overwhelmed. What an abomination. Charlie Brown and Lucy could have put up a better fight than this.